discovering
God's
will

discovering
God's
will

ANDY STANLEY
& REGGIE JOINER

DISCOVERING GOD'S WILL STUDY GUIDE

©2004 by North Point Ministries, Inc.
International Standard Book Number: 978-1-59052-379-7

Cover image by David Muir/Masterfile

Unless otherwise idicated, Scripture quotations are from:
The Holy Bible, New King James Version
©1984 by Thomas Nelson, Inc.
Other Scripture quotations are from:
New American Standard Bible® (NASB) ©1960, 1977, 1995
by the Lockman Foundation. Used by permission.
The Holy Bible, New International Version (NIV)
©1973, 1984 by International Bible Society,
used by permission of Zondervan Publishing House
The Holy Bible, King James Version (KJV)

Published in the United States by Multnomah, an imprint
of the Crown Publishing Group, a division of Penguin Random
House LLC, New York.

MULTNOMAH® and its mountain colophon are registered trademarks
of Penguin Random House LLC.

Printed in the United States of America
2018

25 24 23 22 21 20 19 18 17 16 15

Contents

The Adventure Begins by Andy Stanley
7

Session 1 • Decisions, Decisions…
9

Session 2 • Are You Ready for This?
17

Session 3 • A State of Emergency
27

Session 4 • Getting to the Good Stuff
35

Session 5 • A View from the Top
45

Session 6 • Inside the Mind of God
53

Session 7 • The Big Picture
61

Session 8 • This One Thing
71

Leader's Guide
81

The Adventure Begins

by Andy Stanley

If I had to summarize this series in two points, they would be:

1. God has a personal vision for your life.
2. He wants you to know it even more than you do.

That may come as welcome news. It might even be a complete shock. Because if you're like most people, this isn't the first time you've thought about God's will for your life. It could be one of those nagging questions that follows you through life as you face different decisions. Maybe you've even looked in the Bible before, hoping to unlock God's secret plan for your existence. But that can be frustrating, too. Where do you start? Should you climb a mountain like Moses and expect to get the answer written in stone? Or wait for strange dreams, like Peter, in hopes of finding direction there?

Friends, parents, even church leaders often give conflicting advice—not to mention all the books that have been written on the subject. So how do you know?

As sure as God made you, He also has a vision for how your life will go. He doesn't force it on you, or play tricks on you to see if you'll stray. He stands by, patiently waiting for hearts that will turn to Him with a sincere desire to know His will at any given moment. And since He also invented communication, you can rest assured that when God is ready to give you direction, you can't miss it.

That being said, there are some things *you* can do to get in on the amazing plan God has in mind for your life. I'm looking forward to spending the next several weeks together...*Discovering God's Will!*

Decisions, Decisions...

Introduction

Take a moment to think about where you are today. How would you describe your progress? Is your work (or school) going well? Is it challenging...satisfying... overwhelming? Do you consider yourself successful at this point? Now think about your relationships. Are you where you want to be in your family life? Or with friendships? How are you doing financially? Have you met some key financial goals you set for yourself? Have you experienced any setbacks?

For each of your responses to these questions, you could probably include an explanation of *why* things are the way they are. You may point to certain circumstances that came together to shape the outcome. There may be a person who holds the key to your success or failure in a particular area. Maybe it's a series of breaks, good or bad, that has impacted your situation at the moment. Or perhaps it was just your upbringing in general that set you on an inevitable path in life.

Circumstances and other people have an unmistakable impact on your life, but the focus of this series is on the part *you* control: your decisions. Every person is the product of his or her decisions in life. In fact, your decisions say more about you than any set of circumstances ever will...no matter how good or bad they may be! Helen Keller, Thurgood Marshall, Bill Clinton, Tiger Woods, Howard Hughes some faced overwhelming odds, some received the greatest of opportunities. But in the end, for better or worse, their decisions determined their course in life.

Your life today is the sum total of the decisions you have made. You can try to blame your parents. You can try to blame the government or the economy or your friends. But in the end, you will be measured by *your* part in the decisions you have made. For some people, the focus in life is trying to gain control of their environment. But successful people are those who recognize that we never have complete control over our circumstances. Instead, they focus on making good decisions in spite of limitations.

So how did you end up where you are today? Was it your upbringing? Hard work? Your good looks? In this session, we'll give you a chance to delve a little deeper into the decisions you've made in life so far and gain a deeper understanding of just how *your* choices have impacted your past and will shape your future.

Exercise - How did they do that?

A. In column A below, write down the names of the first three famous people that come to mind. They can be people from the history books, or someone alive today.

A Famous Person	B Noteworthy Characteristic	C Landmark Decision

A man makes decisions. But in the end, those decisions make the man.

B. In column B, beside each of the names above, write a few words to convey something that is noteworthy about him or her. It may be a positive statement or a negative one.

C. In column C, write down at least one decision, for better or for worse, that played a part in making that person noteworthy.

Share your responses with the group.

11

Notes:

Video Notes

From the video message, fill in the blanks.

1. Life is the sum total of the _____ we make.
2. Most people have some _____ about the decisions they've made.
3. _____ wants to direct our lives.
4. Christians often give contrary _____.
5. What you do with your life is of utmost importance to _____.
6. The Bible talks about the _____, _____, and _____ will of God.
7. The _____ will of God refers to those things God is going to do, regardless.
8. God uses _____ and _____ to accomplish his providential will.
9. The _____ will of God refers to the dos and don'ts God has commanded.
10. The _____ will of God refers to personal decisions and plans for our lives.
11. The more _____ you are with the providential will of God, and the more _____ you are to the moral will of God, the easier it will be to discover the personal will of God for your life.
12. God's _____ will and God's _____ will determine the plumb line for everything else God is going to call and ask you to do.

13

Discussion Questions

Take a few moments to discuss your answers to these questions with the group.

1. How would you categorize your desire to know the will of God at this point in your life?
    a. I have a specific issue and I need help making a decision now.
    b. I have made poor decisions in the past, and I'm interested in repairing the damage.
    c. I simply want a good long-term plan for the future.
    d. Not sure.

2. On a scale of 1–10 (10 being always), how much have you taken God's will into consideration when making decisions in life?

14

3. Aside from God, what other sources do people consider before making decisions?

4. Read Mark 12:29–30. What does this passage suggest about God's will for your life?

5. Name at least one way your life might reflect the fulfillment of God's will for your life as suggested in Mark 12:29–30? Give examples.

Mileposts Key Points

✓ Your life is the sum total of your decisions.

✓ The more familiar you become with the pro- vidential will of God, and the more surrendered you become to the moral will of God, the easier it will be to determine the personal will of God for your life.

15

What Will You Do? Assignment for the Week

1. This week, think about the many decisions you make each day from the biggest to the smallest. How do those decisions shape the course of each day? What factors shape your choices? As you observe your daily routine this week, write down at least one area where you would like to become more intentional and strategic in your decision making. _____

2. For the area of concern you listed in question 1 above, find at least one Bible verse that addresses it and write the reference here. _____

Think About It

Does your Bible verse in question 2 deal more with God's providential will or His moral will?

Changing Your Mind Scripture Memory

The more familiar you are with God's ways, the easier it will be to discover His personal will for your life. Begin today to train your mind with the things God says. Then when decision time comes again, you'll be ready.

> *With my whole heart I have sought You; Oh, let me not wander from Your commandments!*
> Psalm 119:10

16

We examined how our lives are the sum total of the decisions we make. We also learned what is meant by the providential, moral, and personal will of God. God's will for your life can always be found somewhere in the intersection of His moral statutes for man and His providential plan for mankind.

Are You Ready for This?

Introduction

Look before you leap. Test the waters. Do your homework. Read the fine print. You've heard it all your life. A person should never make a decision without knowing all the facts, right? It's what your parents taught you. You heard it in grade school. And you've seen the results firsthand. By now it's instinctive: Never commit to something before you know the details.

The same is true about getting advice. You listen to all the suggestions first, *then* use your best judgment and make a decision. Right? Not necessarily. As we'll see in this session, it all depends on whom you're asking for advice.

17

You see, discovering the will of your parents or a friend or a coworker is one thing. But discovering *God's* will is completely different. First of all, God is not in the advice business. He's in the Lordship business. So if you really want to get personal and get

God's take on your situation, you'll discover that He requires something up front first: control. More than He wants people who make good decisions, God wants hearts that are surrendered to Him.

God has an uncanny way of knowing where we stand on this issue. And often, He will withhold information about His will until He detects a willingness on our part to follow through on what He says regardless.

So do you really want to know God's will? Are you truly ready for what He'll say? Or are you just looking for another angle on your situation another opinion to consider before you make up your mind? *Your* answer may determine how well you hear *His*.

Exercise Hearing Test

1. In column A below, list up to three areas of concern for which you desire God's input. These could include specific decisions that concern you or just long-range goals for which you want to ensure success.

A	B	C	
Concern:	Best: Worst:	Uncomfortable Comfortable 1 2 3 4 5 6 7 8 9 10	
Concern:	Best: Worst:	Uncomfortable Comfortable 1 2 3 4 5 6 7 8 9 10	
Concern:	Best: Worst:	Uncomfortable Comfortable 1 2 3 4 5 6 7 8 9 10	

2. In column B, briefly describe the best and worst case scenarios that could result from your choices.

3. In column C, circle a number from 1–10 indicating how comfortable you are submitting to God and letting Him decide your fate, regardless of the outcome.

We receive enlightenment only in proportion as we give ourselves more and more completely to God by humble submission and love.

Thomas Merton

19

Notes:

4. For each of the concerns you listed, can you name at least one aspect of God's moral will or His providential will that might offer a plumb line for your decision?

The more readily you submit to God, the more likely it is that you will hear Him when He speaks

Video Notes

From the video message, fill in the blanks.

1. The problem with knowing God's will is not God's unwillingness to _____ ; the problem is our unwillingness to

    _____ _____.

2. God does not give us direction for

    _____.

3. God gives direction for

    _____.

4. Surrendering to the _____ will of God paves the way to discovery of the _____ will of God.

5. _____ people have a very easy time discerning God's will.

6. God is more interested in your discovering _____ than His will.

7. Your prayer life is at an all-time high when you're making a _____.

8. In the process of trying to know His _____, we get to know _____.

9. God _____ communication. That makes Him the greatest _____.

10. God wants you to know His _____ even more than you _____ to know it.

21

Discussion Questions

Take a few moments to discuss your answers to these questions with the group.

We do not first see and then act; we act and then see. And that is why the man who waits to see clearly before he will believe never starts on the journey.

Thomas Merton

1. Is there a difference between seeking God's advice and pursuing His will? Explain.

2. Which do you think is more difficult: discovering God's will or following through once you know it? Explain.

22

3. Name at least two attributes of God that make Him a desirable source of advice for your life.

4. According to Proverbs 3:5–6, what conditions must be met in order for a person's path to be made obvious?

Mileposts Key Points

✓ God does not give us information for consideration, but for participation.

✓ In the process of discovering God's will, we discover God.

What Will You Do? Assignment for the Week

You take many things for granted in the course of a typical day—assumptions you must make in order to function. For example, you assume the sun will come up, gravity will work, your car will start, lunch will be edible, the pilot won't fall asleep.

1. This week, think about the many ways you already rely on God without even thinking about it. Make a list of the ways God is faithful from the biggest to the smallest.

2. Next, make a list of any times when you've relied on God by choice through prayer and obedient action. This list could begin with your decision to place your faith in Christ for salvation.

Think About It

Finally, list specific concerns for which you desire God's input at this point in your life. For each one, find at least one Bible verse that offers evidence that God will be faithful in this area, as He has been in your life in the past.

Changing Your Mind Scripture Memory

Trusting that God has our best in mind comes more naturally when we rehearse in our minds the ways He has been faithful in the past. Fill your mind with concrete evidence of God's faithfulness by meditating on this week's memory verse throughout the week.

25

> Trust in the LORD with all your heart, and lean not on
> your own understanding; in all your ways acknowledge
> Him, and He will make your paths straight.
>
> Proverbs 3:5–6

session
- 3 -

A State of Emergency

Introduction

Have you ever thought about what you would do if your house were on fire? In a situation like that, you have several options. For example, you could run to the bookshelf and look for something on the topic of firefighting, maybe an entry in the encyclopedia or a home safety book. And assuming you found something you could read everything there is to know about extinguishing fires, then go outside, locate several sections of garden hose, and connect them to a spigot and get to work battling the blaze.

27

Or you could simply pick up the phone and dial 911.

The same is true about discovering God's will. There may be times when you have an emergency and you need to know God's personal will for your life *now*. Sure, you could study the Bible from cover to cover and scour the bookshelf for books about God's providential will and moral will. But what if you don't have time for that? Besides, some situations make it impossible to keep an objective perspective anyway. Decisions can be emotional. The facts may be complicated or over your head. You may not be sure if the Bible says anything at all about your situation.

Good news. For occasions like these, God has given us a very practical way to call for help.

God wants us to discover His will even more than we do. And He often places people around us who can shed valuable insight on our situation. As you learn to be sensitive to this channel of communication, you can soon find yourself getting direct input from God through the advice of people right around you. All you have to do is ask.

Exercise *Who You Gonna Call?*

If you had a critical decision to make, where would you turn for help? In the space below, write down the names of at least ten people whose opinions you value enough that you might turn to them for help with a difficult decision.

1. _____

2. _____

3. _____

4. _____

5. _____

6. _____

7. _____

8. _____

9. _____

10. _____

No man is an island, entire of itself; every man is a piece of the continent, a part of the main.

John Donne

29

Notes:

Video Notes

From the video message, fill in the blanks.

I Kings 12
1. The first king of Israel was a man named

   _____.
2. God replaced Saul with _____.
3. David's son _____ followed him
   as the king of Israel.
4. God prophesied that after Solomon was gone,
   the kingdom would be _____.
5. Jereboam fled to _____ to
   escape Solomon.
6. Rehoboam was King Solomon's
   _____ and was expected to be king.
7. Rehoboam asked the people of Israel to go
   away for _____ days.
8. Then Rehoboam consulted the _____
   who had served his father Solomon.
9. Rehoboam rejected the advice of the elders
   and consulted with the _____ men
   who had grown up with him and were
   _____ him.
10. The king did not _____ to the
    people.
11. One of the primary tools that God is going to
    use in your life to guide you is the
    _____ of other believers.
12. Many times we are forced to make decisions
    about things that are so _____ to
    us we cannot be objective.
13. Emotion has a tendency to _____
    our ability to reason.
14. Oftentimes we are asked to make decisions
    about things that are _____ our
    head.

Discussion Questions

Take a few moments to discuss your answers to these questions with the group.

1. In your opinion, what might Rehoboam's motives have been when he sought advice from the elders that had served his father?

2. What might his motives have been when he sought the advice of his friends?

3. Read Proverbs 3:7. What do you think it means to be "wise in your own eyes"? Give examples.

Mileposts Key Points

✓ Seeking counsel can give you access to valuable information for decision making. The benefits fall into three different categories:

1. Experience from someone who's been there.
2. Objectivity from someone who can see the big picture.
3. Expertise from someone who has more knowledge. .

What Will You Do? Assignment for the Week

Seeking input from other people is part of everyday life. It can be a formal thing, such as approaching a friend for specific advice. Or it can be passive, like noticing which grocery store your neighbor chooses or reading an advertisement in a magazine or getting help from a sales clerk. We rely on input from people around us to make basic everyday decisions.

1. This week, pay attention to the times when you rely on input from other people to influence your decisions.

2. Make a list, writing down at least one occasion per day.

33

Think About It

What correlations can you draw between the types of needs you encounter and the types of people you receive advice from?

Changing Your Mind Scripture Memory

God's Word strongly encourages turning to others with our decisions. Train your mind to this principle by meditating on this week's verse throughout the week.

> *A wise man will hear and increase in learning, and a man of understanding will acquire wise counsel.*
> Proverbs 1:5 (NASB)

We learned that one of the best ways to discover God's will is through the counsel of others. This can be especially helpful if you need to know God's will NOW. Throughout the Bible, there are countless examples of God speaking to His people this way. And whether you're in a hurry to discover God's will or not, it's a good idea to begin surrounding yourself now with wise, experienced friends who can help you.

session
- 4 -

Getting to the Good Stuff

Introduction

Advice is pretty easy to come by. *Good* advice, on the other hand, can be a bit more elusive. Choosing the right source for guidance can mean the difference between leveraging God's principle of wise counsel and getting yourself into an even bigger mess.

Getting counsel from someone else is no guarantee that what you hear is from God. In fact, many well-meaning Christians get advice from the wrong sources and end up worse than before. You probably know of situations where bad advice played a role in creating a dilemma. You may even question the value of this principle because of unpleasant experiences... experiences that all started with bad advice.

But make no mistake about it. God uses the counsel of other people to communicate His will.

So how can you be sure that the advice you get is helpful and not harmful? How can you recognize good advice and avoid suggestions that are misleading? How can you recognize the voice of God in the chorus of people around you?

In this session, we'll reveal some basic guidelines for discovering God's will through the counsel of other people. You don't want just anybody's opinion on your situation; you want God's! By observing just a few pointers, you can confidently distinguish between Godly wisdom and random opinions. And once you do, you'll see that oftentimes discovering God's will is simply a matter of knowing where to turn for advice.

Exercise *Choosing Your Cabinet*

In the last session, you brainstormed names of people whose opinions you value enough to seek their input. In this session, we'll take it a step further. Like a new president carefully selecting his cabinet, discovering God's will for your life is often as practical as choosing the right person for the job. In column A below five major areas of common concerns are listed. In column B, write down the names of one to three people whom you consider to have expertise in the corresponding area and have reached a place in that category you hope to reach someday. This list doesn't have to represent your final choices for your "personal cabinet," but it will get you thinking in the right direction.

There are very few honest friends — the demand is not particularly great.

Marie von
Ebner-Eschenbach

A (Area of concern)	B (Someone I can follow)
Career	1. 2. 3.
Money	1. 2. 3.
Family relationships	1. 2. 3.
Friendships	1. 2. 3.
Spiritual	1. 2. 3.

37

Notes:

Video Notes

From the video message, fill in the blanks.

Choosing the right people:

1. Choose someone who has _____ to lose by telling you the truth.
2. Choose someone who is _____ you want to be in life.
3. If possible, ask more than _____ person.
4. Choose someone you _____ and someone you _____.
5. Go into these conversations sensitive to the fact that God may _____ to you.

Three questions to ask:

6. "Are any of the options I'm considering outside the boundaries of _____?"
7. "What do you think the _____ thing is for me to do?"
8. "What would you _____ if you were me?"

Two primary reasons people don't use this principle:

9. The first reason we don't seek counsel is often because of _____.
10. The second reason we don't seek counsel is because we already _____ what we're going to hear.
11. Great leadership is not about making decisions on your _____; it's about _____ the decision once it's been made.

Discussion Questions

Take a few moments to discuss your answers to these questions with the group.

1. Is it always important to seek advice from someone who has nothing to gain or lose from your decision? Why or why not?

'Tis great confidence in a friend to tell him your faults, greater to tell him his.

Benjamin Franklin

2. What's the difference between someone who has *experience* in an area and someone who has *expertise*? Explain.

40

3. Read Proverbs 12:26. According to this verse, why is it important to be discriminating when choosing your counsel?

Mileposts Key Points

✔ There is no one better to show you the way than the one who has been there before.

✔ Following God is often as simple and practical as following godly men and women.

What Will You Do? Assignment for the Week

Often the most difficult thing about seeking wise counsel is breaking the ice and getting comfortable with this practice. This week, your assignment is to receive input from someone about an issue of your choosing.

1. Select one of your top three areas of concern and commit yourself to finding counsel from at least one outsider. It can be through formal pursuit of someone you identify—perhaps someone you listed in the exercise—or you may receive counsel passively, through unsolicited comments made by a desirable source during casual conversation about your situation.

41

2. Pray first. Then write down the area of concern:

3. Pray also that God would enable you to have a moment of counsel with the right person. If necessary, pursue someone intentionally. Briefly summarize the direction you received through counsel:

Think About It

Think about the results of your pursuit of counsel.

On a scale of 1–10 (10 being most comfortable), how comfortable was the experience?

Was the person receptive to your request?

Did the advice you received closely match what you expected?

Did you like the advice you got?

Do you feel more peace and confidence because of your encounter, or less?

Would it be helpful to get advice from another source before making any decisions?

Changing Your Mind *Scripture Memory*

Turning to others may not come naturally to you. To make God's ways a natural part of life, meditate on what God has to say throughout the week.

> *He who walks with wise men will be wise, but the companion of fools will suffer harm.*
> Proverbs 13:20 (NASB)

43

We examined the importance of being discriminating when asking the advice of others. Almost everyone can offer an opinion of your situation. But godly counsel tends to come from carefully chosen advisers who can lend an element of expertise and objectivity to your situation.

session
- 5 -

A View from the Top

Introduction

It's amazing how much your perspective can change with a little information. As a young child, the idea of allowing the doctor to give you a shot probably didn't make much sense. In fact, it may have taken some parental pressure or bribery to get you to cooperate. You didn't know anything about preventive medicine or what immunization meant. All you knew was that it hurt.

45

Over time, of course, things change. By the time you're an adult, you go to the doctor under your own power. You submit willingly to the same kind of shot. You even *pay* to have it done to you. All because information has altered your perspective.

As a child of God, the same is true. God declares, "So are My ways higher than your ways...my thoughts than your thoughts" (Isaiah 55:9). No matter how old or smart you get, there are some things about life you just won't understand like God does. You don't think as God thinks because you simply don't have the information. His perspective runs across millions of years, and it leaves nothing out of the equation. He has more information than the human brain can hope to contain. That's why it's always better to follow God's intuition rather than our own.

Fortunately, you don't have to *be* God to begin *thinking* like God. God wants to share His intuition with you... to give you a view from the top. And the best picture of His perspective comes from the pages of His Word. His invitation is, "Take My yoke upon you and *learn* from me" (Matthew 11:29). The Bible may not parallel your own situation exactly, but as you learn to study it properly, it offers an invaluable look inside the mind of God. And that's a vital perspective when your goal is discovering God's will.

Exercise *Going Behind the Scenes*

Every decision has the potential to be swayed by fear
and desire. You may fear a bad experience. Or be
overwhelmed by a desire for something. Your intuition can distort your perspective and lead you down
a path that's not the best.

1. Think back over your past. Try to identify one
   to three situations in which a decision you
   made could have been better. It may be something you totally regret or simply a situation
   that left some room for improvement. Describe
   your decision briefly in column 1 below:

1. Decisions I made	2. Fear or desire

2. In column 2, try to identify a fear or a desire
   that may have skewed your perspective and
   hindered your decision-making ability.

Notes:

Video Notes

From the video message, fill in the blanks.

1. The Bible is so _____, there's a tendency to overlook it as a primary tool.
2. The Bible is a _____ means through which God desires to lead us and direct us.
3. David found comfort and counsel in God's _____.
4. We are to use God's Word to find His _____ for our lives.
5. One way would be to look in the _____ and find people who had parallel situations to our own.
6. In making decisions, what is naturally _____ to us may actually lead us astray.
7. Our logic, from God's perspective, may be _____.

The Three Elements of a Decision:

8. There are three things that come to bear on any decision: the context, your perspective, and the _____.
9. Our context is limited to what we know and what we've _____.
10. Our perspective is always impacted by our desires and our _____.
11. The outcome is just a _____.
12. In the Scriptures, what God has given us is a slice of His _____.

Always trust your intuition. Unless, of course, it's wrong.

Anonymous

49

Never use intuition.

General Omar Bradley

Discussion Questions

Take a few moments to discuss your answers to these questions with the group.

1. In our culture, are you more likely to hear messages that encourage you to follow your intuition or to question it?

Intuition is reason in a hurry.

Holbrook Jackson

2. In the Bible, are you more likely to hear messages that encourage you to follow your intuition or to question it?

50

3. Read Psalm 33:1–22. Name one or two attributes of God from this passage that make His perspective superior to man's perspective when it comes to decision-making.

Mileposts Key Points

✓ In making decisions, what is naturally intuitive to us may actually lead us astray.

What Will You Do? Assignment for the Week

Read Job 38:1–42:6.

1. From this passage, identify at least five accomplishments God presents to Job as a reminder of His sovereignty.

2. Next, list five facts about your own life that point to God's sovereignty. It may be a specific way He has intervened in your life or an everyday miracle like your ability to breathe.

51

Think About It

Finally, name three things about God that make Him a sovereign and trustworthy source for your everyday decisions.

Changing Your Mind Scripture Memory

Begin now to train your mind to mirror God's, begin-
ning with this week's verse, which focuses on the
superiority of God's way of thinking.

> *"For My thoughts are not your thoughts, neither are your
> ways My ways," declares the LORD. "For as the heavens
> are higher than the earth, so are My ways higher than
> your ways, and My thoughts than your thoughts."*
> Isaiah 55:8–9 (NASB)

We saw how intuition can be a dangerous thing—even if it appears to draw its direction from Scripture. Just because you can find a passage of Scripture to support a view doesn't mean God is leading you in that direction. Using Scripture to affirm God's will on specific issues requires balance and discernment. And learning God's mind may require more than simply discovering a Bible verse.

session
- 6 -

Inside the Mind of God

Introduction

Psychology has come a long way. Once considered an obscure science practiced mainly by social workers, psychology is now a multibillion-dollar industry. Expensive books and elaborate seminars entice the interest of corporations and executive training programs looking for the competitive edge. Professional athletes rely on sports psychologists to help them get in "the zone." In fact, virtually every top athlete today keeps at least one such clinician on his or her staff. Current conventional wisdom says "Thinking like a winner is the first step to performing like one." Numerous lengthy studies have confirmed the link between a person's thought process and his performance. NFL quarterback Roger Staubach summarized his Hall of Fame career, "Every time I stepped on the field, I believed my team was going to walk off the winner, somehow, some way."

53

Without a doubt, what you *think* determines how you *act*. As the writer of Proverbs observed, "For as he thinketh in his heart, so is he" (Proverbs 23:7, KJV).

Just as thinking like a winner is tantamount to performing like one, learning to think like God is the first step toward making godly decisions. In the last session, we exposed the frailties of human intuition, suggesting that God's intuition is a much better guide for making decisions about life. In this session, we'll identify some strategies for modeling your thought processes after God's. The better you understand the mind of God, the easier it will be to determine His will for your life.

The Bible is our best blueprint for understanding how God thinks. From pages and pages of stories, commands, and promises, key principles begin to emerge that point us toward the values God holds dear. We get clues about His desires, preferences, and priorities. We are reminded of His ultimate mission. And we begin to see ourselves as main characters in a play He has written. Becoming familiar with God's principles will allow you to see beyond confusing circumstances or heated emotions, so that you can interpret God's will in any given situation.

54

Exercise Name That Principle

One of the most important skills you can develop is learning to identify principles from God's Word. Sometimes the principle may be stated, sometimes it may only be implied, and other times it is illustrated through a parable or a story. In this exercise, we'll practice identifying God's principles in the Scriptures. Have someone read aloud the passage indicated in column A. Then in column B create your own name for the principle(s) you identify from the passage, and give a brief explanation to describe it. An example is provided below.

Without God's Word, we are guided only by our fears and our desires.

A Passage	B Principle
Galatians 6:7–8	*The Principle of Sowing and Reaping*– You reap what you sow; every action has a resulting outcome; as a general rule, a person should expect the outcome to reflect what he has sown to create it.
Proverbs 3:9–10	
Proverbs 28:19	
Matthew 25:34–40	

55

Notes:

Video Notes

From the video message, fill in the blanks.

1. We have the opportunity, the honor, and the privilege to _____ our minds and our thinking so that we think more like God.

2. Three areas where God's ways are higher than ours:
   a. _____
   b. _____
   c. _____ life

3. In our thinking and in our praying, we've got to begin the _____-making process with this presupposition: My ways are not His ways, and my thoughts are not His thoughts.

4. A principle is an _____ truth.

5. Sometimes they describe a cause-and-effect _____.

6. At other times they predict the _____ of behaviors and attitudes.

7. You can disobey _____, but you don't disobey a principle.

Three Ways to Find Principles in the Scriptures:

8. Sometimes principles are _____.

9. Sometimes principles are just _____.

10. Sometimes principles are _____ through narratives.

11. The more familiar we become with the principles of God's Word, the easier it is to discern the _____ of God.

12. Every single decision you make is going to _____ with one of the principles of God's Word.

57

Discussion Questions

Take a few moments to discuss your answers to these questions with the group.

You can't break a principle, but you can break yourself against a principle.

1. When we are not guided by God's principles, we typically resort to whatever our fears and desires lead us to do. What are some ways a person's fears might influence decision making? Give examples.

2. What are some ways a person's desires might influence decision making? Give examples.

58

3. Read Matthew 16:24. What does this passage suggest about the relationship between following God and discovering His will? Explain.

Mileposts Key Points

✔ The Bible is a blueprint for God's mind.
✔ The more familiar you are with God's ways, the
   easier it is to discern His will for your life.

What Will You Do? Assignment for the Week

1. Identify at least one decision you make in the
   course of the week and describe it briefly in the
   space below. It can be a major issue or a minor
   one.

2. Next, identify at least one corresponding principle
   from God's Word that applies to your decision.
   Write the passage and the principle in the space
   provided:

59

Think About It

Was the decision you made driven primarily by a principle from God's Word or more by ordinary fears or desires? Proverbs 19:20 says, "Listen to counsel and receive instruction, that you may be wise in your latter days" (NKJV). In other words, developing a thorough knowledge of God's ways doesn't happen overnight. It takes time. Like a saving's account, the best strategy is to make steady contributions over the long-term. Why not set a personal goal for identifying new principles from God's Word? You might aim for one new nugget of truth per week or per day. Before long, you will find it easier and easier to discern God's will for your life.

Changing Your Mind *Scripture Memory*

God's principles flow naturally only when they become intrinsically linked with our everyday thinking. Meditating on Scripture is the best way to align your thinking with God's thinking.

60

> *Do not conform any longer to the pattern of this world,*
> *but be transformed by the renewing of your mind. Then*
> *you will be able to test and approve what God's will is—*
> *his good, pleasing and perfect will.*
>
> Romans 12:2 (NIV)

Last week...

We examined the proper way to use Scripture in discovering God's will. Finding a verse to support your point of view is a dangerous practice. However, renewing your mind to crucial verses that frame God's principles is the key to learning the mind of God. And knowing God's mind is the first step to understanding His will.

The Big Picture

Introduction

So far, we have identified four main avenues through which God indicates His will for your life. In review, they are:

1. God's providential will
2. God's moral will
3. The counsel of other people
4. God's Word, the Bible

We have said that important clues about God's personal will for your life can be found by paying particular attention to these areas. In fact, discovering God's will is often a matter of knowing how to look for evidence in the right places. These four areas are great places to start.

There are many other areas to search for evidence as well. For example, God often directs us through the authorities He places in our lives. You could also examine your areas of giftedness as an indication of how you should apply yourself. Your opportunities can also be indicators of God's leading. The list goes on.

But there's one area in particular that sort of pulls everything together. This one category has a way of summarizing all the other factors in the equation. When you identify the thumbprint of God in this one area, many questions you might have about God's will for your life in the other areas will be answered. This area is called *vision*. A vision is a personal burden that grows into a mental picture of the way things could be someday. When someone develops a vision, there is a level of unrest over the way things are and a personal conviction to see them become what they could be, what they *should* be. A vision may not always include all the details, but it conveys the big picture. Once consumed with the pursuit of a vision, a person can negotiate the details with clarity and conviction.

Often people find that their gifts, their opportunities in life, their personal resources, and all other indicators will be in alignment with their overall vision. Once you identify a big-picture vision of God's will for your life, it becomes much simpler and easier to discover His will for the details along the way.

Exercise *I Have a Dream* (5–10 minutes)

Have you ever been compelled by a vision? Have you ever had a glimpse of how things *could* be and then worked diligently to move things in that direction? Perhaps you've had this experience with a school assignment, a project at work, or a relationship you've pursued. What about a vision for your life in general? In the space below, write a few statements that describe your vision for your life. This is only an exercise to get the juices flowing, so don't worry if it doesn't perfectly capture all your desires. Picture your life. Write down whatever visions come to mind. Feel free to speak about the future in the present tense, as if it has already come to pass. Try to come up with at least three to five statements about your life. Example statements are provided.

The soul never thinks without a picture.

Aristotle

Vision is the art of seeing things invisible.

Jonathan Swift

Prayer: *Heavenly Father, I want to know Your will. Please begin now to give me a vision of Your will for my life. I ask this in Jesus' name.*

My Dreams:
Example: "I have a vision of using my experience as a medical professional to begin a medical missions ministry for lower-income families."
Example: "I have a vision of enjoying devotional time with my spouse regularly and of being coanchors for each other's spiritual growth."

63

Notes:

Video Notes

From the video message, fill in the blanks.

1. One of the primary ways that God will direct you and guide you in life is by giving you a big-picture _____ for your life.

2. A vision is basically a _____.

3. A vision is a mental image of what could be, fueled by the _____ that this is something that should be true of your life.

4. As the vision gets _____, the options get _____, and the decision gets

    _____.

5. Everybody has some _____ idea of where they want to end up in life.

6. As long as your vision is general, it is not

    _____.

7. Only in the arenas where we have some semblance of a big _____ do the options clarify themselves.

8. As a Christian, as you allow God to have _____ into this picture, it makes discerning His will so much easier.

65

Discussion Questions

Take a few moments to discuss your answers to these questions with the group.

1. In which of the following categories are you personally most likely to have a vision? Rank them in order.

    ___ Career

    ___ Relationship with spouse

    ___ Friendships

    ___ Finances

    ___ Spiritual

2. Have you ever been involved in a task that had a clear vision? Explain.

3. Why is it important to write out goals or visions?

4. Read Ephesians 2:10. What does this passage say about God's vision for your life?

Mileposts Key Points

✔ God uses personal vision to reveal His will.
✔ The clearer the vision, the easier the decision.

What Will You Do? Assignment for the Week

In the exercise for this session, you took a shot at describing your vision for your life. Now let's go a step further. The more specific your vision, the more valuable it is for decision making, helping you to differentiate true opportunities from distractions. For each of the categories below, write a one to three sentence vision statement for that specific area of life. Include as many specific details as you'd like to adequately describe your vision. This is an exercise, so be careful not to "edit" your thoughts too much.

Prayer: *Heavenly Father, once again I am seeking Your help as I attempt to discover Your will for my life. Inspire me now with a vision for specific areas of my life as You begin to unfold Your desires for me. In Jesus' name, amen.*

My Vision

Spiritual:

Marital:

Relational–Family:

Professional:

Financial:

Other:

Think About It

God knows your desires. As your heavenly Father, He is at work in you to transform your character to be like Christ's. Through that process, your desires will begin to reflect His perfect will. As you humble yourself before God and submit to His lordship for your life, you can look for Him to use the desires of your heart to lead you toward His will for your life. As the psalmist wrote: "Delight yourself in the LORD and he will give you the desires of your heart" (Psalm 37:4, NIV).

Changing Your Mind *Scripture Memory*

Your heart can reflect God's true desires for your life. It can also deceive you into selfishness and sin. That's why it's important to hide God's Word continually in your heart.

> *Where there is no vision, the people perish.*
> Proverbs 29:18 (NIV)

We saw how God often reveals His will through something called vision. This is not to be confused with seeing a vision. Vision is a mental image of what could be true in your life, fueled by the conviction that it should be true in your life. The clearer your sense of vision, the fewer your options and the easier your decisions.

session
- 8 -

This One Thing

Introduction

It's one of the shortest words in the English language, but sometimes the word *no* can be one of the most difficult to utter. And if you're not careful, you can end up overbusy and underfulfilled all because you've said yes to everything without first understanding God's vision for your life.

Let's face it, turning someone down is uncomfortable. We don't want to disappoint anybody. We're afraid we might miss an opportunity. What will everyone think? We might feel guilty. Even when we're not being asked, our tendency is often to seek out new areas of interest and become involved.

71

Then there's Nehemiah. His example in the Scriptures is a model of someone discovering God's will and pursuing it with laser accuracy. Rather than agree to any opportunity that came along, Nehemiah was in pursuit of a vision. And his vision enabled him to make even the most monumental decisions with conviction and clarity. Needless to say, Nehemiah knew how to say no.

So what about your life? Is it defined by strategic opportunities or mounting clutter? Do the activities on your calendar point to a long-term goal? Or do they just mark the dates of all the invitations you've received? Once you get a glimpse of God's vision for your life, you will see your options and opportunities in a whole new light. And you'll find it easier than ever to make decisions as you discover God's will.

Exercise *Random activities*

Being spontaneous has its value. But it's no substitute for having a plan. Oddly enough, many of our most time-consuming activities can be traced back to an unplanned encounter. Someone invites you to play tennis, and the next thing you know you're spending twenty hours a week as the captain of your neighborhood tennis team. You're asked to volunteer for a local charity, and before long it's a weekly commitment. It sounds good. But is it a calling from God? From your own experience, can you identify any areas of involvement that began with one of these passive, unplanned encounters? Perhaps you've turned some down. Try to think of three to five examples and list them below:

You've got to be careful if you don't know where you're going, because you might not get there.

Yogi Berra

73

Notes:

Video Notes

From the video message, fill in the blanks.

1. Nehemiah was the cupbearer to a king whose predecessors had destroyed _____.
2. Nehemiah was about _____ miles away from Jerusalem.
3. A vision begins as a _____.
4. Nehemiah began to develop a vision for rebuilding the _____ around Jerusalem.
5. Other _____ in the area were threatened by Nehemiah's plans.
6. Sanballat and his followers invited Nehemiah to meet them on the plain of _____.
7. Nehemiah's response can be translated: "I am doing a great _____, and I cannot come down."
8. For Nehemiah, anything that contributed to rebuilding the wall was a _____, and anything that would distract him from rebuilding the wall was a _____.

Three Points of Application:

9. _____ that God will give you a vision for your life.
10. _____ it down.
11. _____ accordingly.

75

Discussion Questions

Take a few moments to discuss your answers to these questions with the group.

1. Which of the following best describes how you ended up in your current job or occupation?

    •   Where I am today is part of a strategic plan I devised two or more jobs ago.

    •   I have a plan for exactly what the next step in my career/occupation will be.

    •   I have a general sense that this job will lead me where I want to go in life.

    •   This job was a better offer than my last one, so I took it.

    •   I have no idea why I'm here.

2. Read Nehemiah 1:4. What was Nehemiah's first reaction to the news about the remnant in Jerusalem?

3. According to this passage, what did Nehemiah do before presenting his vision to God?

4. Read Nehemiah 2:1–5. What events did God use to give Nehemiah confirmation about his vision?

Mileposts Key Points

✓ Nehemiah modeled the pursuit of a vision in rebuilding the wall around Jerusalem.

✓ The greater the burden, the stronger the conviction and the clearer the vision.

✓ If an opportunity does not fit a specific *mission*, you may be entertaining a *distraction*.

What Will You Do? Assignment for the Week

A vision begins as a burden. The greater the burden, the stronger the conviction and the clearer the vision. This week, think about the things that burden or concern you. When you look at the world around you, are you compelled by the way things *could be* or *should be*? Is there something you long to see happen? To begin understanding the kinds of visions God might want you to pursue in life, examine your burdens. In the space below, write down three to five specific things that you consider a burden, or at least a concern:

Prayer: *Heavenly Father, You know my heart and You created me in Christ for good works that You have prepared beforehand for me to perform. Please help me now to recall specific burdens and concerns that would help me to develop vision for my life. I pray this in Jesus' name, amen.*

Think About It

In the last session, you took a shot at describing a vision for different areas of your life. Based on the burdens you wrote down above, are there any things you should add to the vision statements you drafted? For each burden you mentioned above, rewrite a corresponding one to three sentence vision statement in the appropriate categories.

Spiritual:

Marital:

Relational–Family:

Professional:

Financial:

Other:

Changing Your Mind Scripture Memory

Having a vision for your life is one thing, but having a God-given vision for your life is what you really want. The more familiar you are with the heart of God, the greater the likelihood that God will birth a vision in your heart. Meditating on His Word can help.

> *Be very careful, then, how you live—not as unwise but as wise, making the most of every opportunity, because the days are evil. Therefore do not be foolish, but understand what the Lord's will is.*
>
> Ephesians 5:15–17 (NIV)

discovering God's will

Leader's Guide

Basics About Leading

So you're the leader! Is that intimidating? Perhaps just exciting? No doubt you have some mental pictures of what it will look like what you will say and how it will go. Before you get too far into the planning process, there are some things you should know about leading a small-group discussion. We've compiled some tried and true techniques here to help you.

1. Don't teach ...facilitate—Perhaps you've been part of a Sunday school class or Bible study in which the leader could answer any question and always had something interesting to say. It's easy to think you need to be like that, too. Relax. You don't. Leading a small group is quite different. Instead of being the featured act at the party, think of yourself as the host or hostess behind the scenes. Your primary job is to create an environment where people feel comfortable and to keep the meeting generally on track. Your party is most successful when your guests do most of the talking.

2. Cultivate discussion— It's also easy to think that the meeting lives or dies by *your* ideas. In reality, what makes a small-group meeting successful are the ideas of everyone in the group. The most valuable thing you can do is to get people to share their thoughts. That's how the relationships in your group will grow and thrive. Here's a rule: The impact of your study material will typically never exceed the impact of the relationships through which it was studied. The more meaningful the relationships, the more meaningful the study. In a sterile environment even the best material is suppressed.

3. Point to the material —A good host or hostess gets the party going by offering delectable hors d'oeuvres and

83

beverages. You too should be ready to serve up "delicacies" from the material. Sometimes you will simply read the discussion questions and invite everyone to respond. At other times, you may encourage others to share their own ideas: Remember, some of the best treats are the ones your guests will bring to the party. Go with the flow of the meeting, and be ready to pop out of the kitchen as needed.

4. Depart from the material   —A talented ministry team has carefully designed this study for your small group. But that doesn't mean you should follow every part word for word. Knowing how and when to depart from the material is a valuable art. Nobody knows more about your people than you do. The narratives, questions, and exercises are here to provide a framework for discovery. However, every group is motivated differently. Sometimes the best way to start a small-group discussion is simply to ask, "Does anyone have any personal insights or revelations you'd like to share from this week's material?" Then sit back and listen.

5. Stay on track   —Conversation is the currency of a small group discussion. The more interchange, the healthier the "economy." However, you need to keep your objectives in mind. If your goal is to have a meaningful experience with this material, then you should make sure the discussion is contributing to that end. It's easy to get off on a tangent. Be prepared to interject politely and refocus the group. You may need to say something like, "Excuse me, we're obviously all interested in this subject; however, I just want to make sure we cover all the material for this week."

6. Above all, pray   —The best communicators are the ones who manage to get out of God's way enough to let Him communicate *through* them. That's important to keep in mind. Books don't teach God's Word; neither do sermons or group discussions. God Himself speaks into the hearts of men and women, and prayer is our vital channel to communicate directly with Him. So cover your efforts in prayer. You don't just want God present at your meeting; you want Him to direct it.

ADDITIONAL CONVERSATION STARTERS: At the end of each week's discussion questions in the leader's guide section, you will find additional questions that you may choose to use to prompt discussion in your group. These questions do not appear in the main workbook sessions. You don't have to use these questions at all. Or you may choose one or two that best suit the personalities and interests of your group. The purpose of these questions is to give you additional material to help create a fun, exciting, and meaningful discussion time with your group. NOTE: There is also a section entitled "additional suggestions" at the end of each session in the leader's guide, which you may also choose to introduce to your group.

We hope you find these suggestions helpful, and we hope you enjoy leading this study. You will find additional guides and suggestions for each session in the leader's guide notes that follow.

Leader' Guide Session Notes

SESSION 1   *Decisions, Decisions...*

KEY POINT: *People are the product of the decisions they make. The essence of free will is having the choice to seek God's desires or pursue some other path. Discovering God's will is the first step toward making decisions that are beneficial and productive.*

EXERCISE:
The point of this exercise is to demonstrate that a person's legacy is determined primarily by the decisions he or she makes, more so oftentimes than by the circumstances he or she faces or the accomplishments he or she achieves.

VIDEO NOTES:
1. Life is the sum total of the <u>decisions</u> we make.
2. Most people have some <u>regrets</u> about the decisions they've made.
3. <u>God</u> wants to direct our lives.
4. Christians often give contrary <u>advice</u>.
5. What you do with your life is of utmost importance to <u>God</u>.
6. The Bible talks about the <u>providential</u>, <u>moral</u>, and <u>personal</u> will of God.
7. The <u>providential</u> will of God refers to those things God is going to do, regardless.
8. God uses <u>men</u> and <u>women</u> to accomplish his providential will.
9. The <u>moral</u> will of God refers to the dos and don'ts God has commanded.
10. The <u>personal</u> will of God refers to personal decisions and plans for our lives.
11. The more <u>familiar</u> you are with the providential will of God and the more <u>surrendered</u> you are to the moral will of God, the easier it will be to discover the personal will of God for your life.
12. God's <u>providential</u> will and God's <u>moral</u> will determine the plumb line for everything else God is going to call and ask you to do.

NOTES FOR DISCUSSION QUESTIONS:

1. How would you categorize your desire to know the will of God at this point in your life?
   a. I have a specific issue and I need help making a decision now.
   b. I have made poor decisions in the past, and I'm interested in repairing the damage.
   c. I simply want a good long-term plan for the future.
   d. Not sure.
      The purpose of this question is to pique people's interest in discovering God's will.

2. On a scale of 1–10 (10 being always), how much have you taken God's will into consideration when making decisions in life?
   The purpose of this question is to encourage people to examine their sensitivity to God's will.

3. Aside from God, what sources do people consider before making decisions?
   The purpose of this question is to point out the messages that compete for our attention and obscure both our concern for and understanding of God's will.

4. Read Mark 12:29–30. What does this passage suggest about God's will for your life?
   God's will for our lives will always centers around the basic mission of loving Him completely—heart, mind, soul, and strength.

ADDITIONAL CONVERSATION STARTERS:

5. Name one example of God's providential will.
   The purpose of this question is to ensure a basic understanding of the term "providential will."

6. Name one example of God's moral will.
   The purpose of this question is to ensure a basic understanding of the term "moral will."

7. Name one example of God's personal will for your life.
   The purpose of this question is to ensure a basic understanding of the term "personal will."

8. In your own words, briefly describe God's providential will— that is, what He's up to in the world today.
   What goals does He have for mankind? For Himself?
   The purpose of this question is to encourage people to realize how God's providential will is being carried out even today.

9. Name at least one way your life might help God accomplish His providential will in the world.
   The purpose of this question is to encourage people to begin thinking in terms of making decisions that are in alignment with God's providential will.

10. If you had to pick only one, which of the following areas in your life has been most impacted by your attention, or lack of attention, to God's moral will?
    a. Work/school/career
    b. Family
    c. Finances
    d. Friendships
    The purpose of this question is to create a deeper realization of how our observance of God's moral will can impact our lives.

11. What are some common factors that distract us from basing our decisions on God's providential and moral will?
    Similar to question 3, this question is intended to help people begin to identify the enemies of their success so that they may eventually be neutralized.

WHAT WILL YOU DO?
The goal of this assignment is to underscore the concept of searching God's Word for principles to guide the decision-making process.

ADDITIONAL SUGGESTIONS:
Ask your group this question: At what point are decisions so small that it is not really necessary to formally seek God's will?

SESSION 2 *Are You Ready for This?*

KEY POINT: *The goal of this session is to create a clear distinction between desiring to follow God's will and desiring to benefit from His wisdom. God doesn't give advice; He gives direction. But He only gives it to hearts that are first surrendered to His lordship. If you're looking for opinions, ask your friends. If you're looking to give God control of your life, you're essentially guaranteed to find out His will in the process.*

EXERCISE:
The point of this exercise is to encourage people to become aware of how receptive they are to the idea of giving God control of their lives.

VIDEO NOTES:
From the video message, fill in the blanks:

1. The problem with knowing God's will is not God's unwillingness to <u>speak</u>; the problem is our unwillingness to <u>follow through</u>.
2. God does not give us direction for <u>consideration</u>.
3. God gives direction for <u>participation</u>.
4. Surrender to the <u>known</u> will of God paves the way to discovery of the <u>unknown</u> will of God.
5. <u>Broken</u> people have a very easy time discerning God's will.
6. God is more interested in your discovering <u>Him</u> than His will.
7. Your prayer life is at an all-time high when you're making a <u>decision</u>.
8. In the process of trying to know His <u>will</u>, we get to know <u>Him</u>.
9. God <u>created</u> communication. That makes Him the greatest <u>communicator</u>.
10. God wants you to know His <u>will</u> even more than you <u>want</u> to know it.

NOTES FOR DISCUSSION QUESTIONS:

1. Is there a difference between seeking God's advice and pursuing His will? Explain.
   The purpose of this question is to encourage people to analyze whether their desire is to follow God's will or simply to benefit from His wisdom.
2. Which do you think is more difficult: discovering God's will or following through once you know it? Explain.
   There is no right or wrong answer here. This question is designed to call attention to the importance of acting on the "known" will of God.

89

3. Name at least two attributes of God that make Him a desirable source of advice for your life.
   Following up on question 1, this question is designed to remind us that God is trustworthy, faithful, and capable to direct our lives.

4. According to Proverbs 3:5–6, what conditions must be met in order for a person's path to be made obvious?
   This question reiterates the concept of surrendering first, then learning God's will. Answers might include: trusting God with all your heart, not trusting in your own ideas, acknowledging His lordship in all areas of life, etc.

ADDITIONAL CONVERSATION STARTERS:

5. If you had to accept God's will before it was revealed, what would you think was the worst thing He might make you do?
   The goal of this question is to expose some of the fears that prevent us from surrendering completely to God.

6. What would be the greatest thing God might make you do?
   Similar to question 3, this question reminds us that God's plans are not to harm us but to give us a future and a hope.

7. Describe two or three everyday situations in which you submit to the will of another person or authority without knowing all the details.
   The goal of this question is to create the realization that we surrender control to people other than God all the time. Some answers might include: flying on an airplane in which a pilot is in control, going to the doctor, the workplace, etc.

8. Of the examples you listed above, which ones are you most comfortable with? Why?
   The point of this question is to demonstrate that while we all have our preferences, the concept of surrendering control is the same.

WHAT WILL YOU DO?
This assignment should demonstrate that relying on God is something people do whether they realize it or not. Simply drawing a breath of air presumes innumerable microscopic functions inside the human body—all created and sustained by God. If we trust God for those things without a thought, then trusting Him with other areas should come just as naturally.

ADDITIONAL SUGGESTIONS:
Ask your group this question: Why do you think people tend to resist the idea of giving God complete control of their lives?

SESSION 3 *A State of Emergency*

KEY POINT: *God reveals His will through practical means. Often it is as easy as seeking counsel from the people around us. The story of Rehoboam suggests both the positive and negative potential of this principle.*

EXERCISE:
This exercise is intended to get people thinking about whom they might ask for counsel; moreover, the exercise might demonstrate that help is more readily available than one might first imagine.

VIDEO NOTES:
From the video message, fill in the blanks.
1. The first king of Israel was a man named <u>Saul</u>.
2. God replaced Saul with <u>David</u>.
3. David's son <u>Solomon</u> followed him as the king of Israel.
4. God prophesied that after Solomon was gone, the kingdom would be <u>divided</u>.
5. Jereboam fled to <u>Egypt</u> to escape Solomon.
6. Rehoboam was King Solomon's <u>son</u> and was expected to be king.
7. Rehoboam asked the people of Israel to go away for <u>three</u> days.
8. Then Rehoboam consulted the <u>elders</u> who had served his father Solomon.
9. Rehoboam rejected the advice of the elders and consulted with the <u>young</u> men who had grown up with him and were <u>serving</u> him.
10. The king did not <u>listen</u> to the people.
11. One of the primary tools that God is going to use in your life to guide you is the <u>counsel</u> of other believers.
12. Many times we are forced to make decisions about things that are so <u>close</u> to us we cannot be objective.
13. Emotion has a tendency to <u>cloud</u> our ability to reason.
14. Oftentimes we are asked to make decisions about things that are <u>over</u> our heads.

NOTES FOR DISCUSSION QUESTIONS:
1. In your opinion, what might Rehoboam's motives have been when he sought advice from the elders that had served his father?

91

There are no right or wrong answers here. The main point is to help us identify with Rehoboam and compare his situation to our own.

2. What might his motives have been when he sought the advice of his friends?

   As in question 1, we should be able to imagine personal situations that might parallel Rehoboam's significance.

3. Read Proverbs 3:7. What do you think it means to be "wise in your own eyes"? Give examples.

   The main point here is to prompt thoughtful consideration about how well we listen for God versus following our own intuition or "conventional" wisdom.

ADDITIONAL CONVERSATION STARTERS:

4. Can you name one situation from your past when you sought advice from someone to help you make a decision? Did it help?

   Chances are, people already use this principle without giving it much thought. The goal of this session is for people to learn to use it intentionally as well.

5. In which of the following types of situations would you be most comfortable seeking counsel? Rank them in order by numbering them 1–5 (1 being most comfortable). Discuss your responses.

   • Advice about a close relationship
   • Help with personal finances
   • Guidance about a difficult situation at work
   • Questions about spiritual/religious issues
   • Family-related matters

   Seeking counsel can be uncomfortable. This exercise is designed to break the ice and encourage people to visualize the process and become familiar with the idea in different situations.

6. In which of these areas are you most likely to need counsel? Rank them by numbering them 1–5 (1 being most likely). Discuss your responses.

   __ Close relationships
   __ Personal finances
   __ Situation at work
   __ Spiritual questions
   __ Family relationships

   The point of this exercise is to encourage people to become familiar with their need for counsel in different areas.

7. Which of the following factors is most likely to keep you from seeking advice when you need it? Rank them by numbering them 1–5 (1 being most likely). Discuss your responses.

__ Embarrassed to ask
__ Too preoccupied to think of asking
__ Afraid to admit need
__ Don't want to impose
__ Don't know whom to ask

The purpose of this question is to help people identify obstacles in hopes of neutralizing them eventually.

8. When seeking counsel, what are some advantages of turning to someone who knows you?
The point of this question is to elicit thought about the pros and cons of different potential sources of counsel.

9. What are some advantages of turning to someone who doesn't know you?
Like question 8, the point of this question is to elicit thought about the pros and cons of different potential sources of counsel.

10. In your opinion, is it possible to get direction from God through the advice of non-Christians? Explain.
The main point here is that God's direction can come in various forms, and that the person giving counsel may be unaware that God is using him to guide you. For example, good medical counsel can come from the professional wisdom of a trained doctor, whether Christian or not. God is powerful enough to speak directly to you in any situation, using any source.

WHAT WILL YOU DO?
There is a tendency to believe seeking counsel is always a formal procedure. The point of this exercise is to illustrate that most people already seek counsel…it's a normal part of everyday life. That being the case, it only takes some minor modifications to begin using this principle to discover God's will.

ADDITIONAL SUGGESTIONS:
Ask your group this question: Why do you think God chooses to speak to us through the advice of others?

SESSION 4 *Getting to the Good Stuff*

KEY POINT: *Just because a person seeks counsel, it's no guarantee that God is speaking. There are a few guidelines for choosing the right people and asking the right kinds of questions.*

EXERCISE:
The purpose of this exercise is to get people thinking more specifically about how they would implement this principle in everyday life. By visualizing it in greater detail, they move one step closer to making it a common practice.

VIDEO NOTES:
From the video message, fill in the blanks.
1. Choose someone who has <u>nothing</u> to lose by telling you the truth.
2. Choose someone who is <u>where</u> you want to be in life.
3. If possible, ask more than <u>one</u> person.
4. Choose someone you <u>know</u> and someone you <u>don't</u> know.
5. Go into these conversations sensitive to the fact that God may <u>speak</u> to you.

Three questions to ask:
6. Ask, "Are any of the options I'm considering outside the boundaries of <u>Scripture</u>?"
7. Ask, "What do you think the <u>best</u> thing is for me to do?"
8. Ask, "What would you <u>do</u> if you were me?"

Two primary reasons people don't use this principle:
9. The first reason we don't seek counsel is often because of <u>pride</u>.
10. The second reason we don't seek counsel is because we already <u>know</u> what we're going to hear.
11. Great leadership is not about making decisions on your <u>own</u>, it's about <u>owning</u> the decisions once they have been made.

NOTES FOR DISCUSSION QUESTIONS:
1. Is it always important to seek advice from someone who has nothing to gain or lose from your decision? Why or why not?
   Obviously, advice will be more objective when it is not obscured by someone else's agenda. The point of this question is to foster a realization of just how much someone's advice might be altered by subconscious motives.
2. What's the difference between someone who has *experience* in an area and someone who has *expertise*? Explain.

94

Experience is no guarantee of expertise. For example, just because someone has been married several times doesn't mean her or she is qualified to be a marriage counselor.

3. Read Proverbs 12:26. According to this verse, why is it important to be discriminating when choosing your counsel?
The outcome of your decision may depend on the wisdom of the counsel you choose.

ADDITIONAL CONVERSATION STARTERS:

4. If you could choose only one person for counsel, who do you think would be more beneficial: someone who knows you or someone who doesn't? Explain.
In reality, one is not universally better than the other. This question is intended to point out that both types can have their benefits. It depends on the situation.

5. Is someone "ahead of you" in life always older? Explain.
The answer is no. This question is intended to encourage people to rehearse the various qualities that make for valuable counselors.

6. The Bible says, "For the foolishness of God is wiser than man's wisdom" (I Corintians 1:25). Are there times when man's wisdom might be God's way of speaking to you? Explain.
While God's ways are higher than man's, His method of revealing them is sometimes quite practical and down-to-earth. Good old common sense is yet another way God might reveal His will.

7. In your opinion, what is the most uncomfortable part of asking for guidance from someone you respect?
This question is designed to confront specific obstacles that might prevent someone from implementing the principle of seeking counsel.

8. When you are in a leadership position, could seeking counsel ever be perceived as a weakness? Discuss.
This question is intended to disarm the notion that a leader is weak because he looks outside for decision-making help.

WHAT WILL YOU DO?

This exercise can be very challenging for some people. Be sensitive, but don't let people off the hook completely. No matter how uncomfortable it feels to seek counsel, the rewards of knowing God's will might be waiting on the other side. The goal of this assignment is to encourage people to step out and begin accessing this vital communication channel.

ADDITIONAL SUGGESTIONS:

Ask your group this question: What are some ways your world would be different if you were never permitted to seek counsel?

SESSION 5 *A View from the Top*

KEY POINT: *Intuition can be a valuable guide. But intuition can also be wrong! God's intuition, however, is always right. And it's mapped out for us in the pages of the Bible. The more familiar you become with God's Word, the more you will begin to think as He thinks and choose as He would choose.*

EXERCISE:
If we don't embrace and apply God's Word and His ways, then most of our decisions will be driven by our fears and our desires. This point often becomes obvious through a simple examination of a person's past experiences. The goal of this exercise is to cultivate the resolve that future decisions will be based on God's principles, not on fears and desires.

VIDEO NOTES:
From the video message, fill in the blanks.
1. The Bible is so <u>misused</u> that there's a tendency to overlook it as a primary tool.
2. The Bible is a <u>primary</u> means through which God desires to lead us and direct us.
3. David found comfort and counsel in God's <u>Word</u>.
4. We are to use God's Word to find His <u>will</u> for our lives.
5. One way would be to look in the <u>Bible</u> and find people who had parallel situations to our own.
6. In making decisions, what is naturally <u>intuitive</u> to us may actually lead us astray.
7. Our logic, from God's perspective, may be <u>illogical</u>.

The Three Elements of a Decision:
8. There are three things that come to bear on any decision: the context, your perspective, and the <u>outcome</u>.
9. Our context is limited to what we know and what we've <u>experienced</u>.
10. Our perspective is always impacted by our desires and our <u>fears</u>.
11. The outcome is just a <u>guess</u>.
12. In the Scriptures, what God has given us is a slice of His <u>thinking</u>.

NOTES FOR DISCUSSION QUESTIONS:
1. In our culture, are you more likely to hear messages that encourage you to follow your intuition or to question it?

It is commonplace to hear the suggestion "Go with your gut feeling." This question is intended to expose and refute such advice.

2. In the Bible, are you more likely to hear messages that encourage you to follow your intuition or to question it?
Like question 1, this question points to the fact that the Bible warns about the frailties of human intuition. Only as it is aligned with God's Word is it reliable as a decision-making aid.

3. Read Psalms 33:1–22. Name one or two attributes of God from this passage that make His perspective superior to man's perspective when it comes to decision making.
This can be a powerful experience for the group. God's perspective is so superior to man's that there's no comparing the two. But unless we rehearse the facts about God frequently, we can lose sight of His omnipotence. This exercise is designed to bring us face-to-face with the Creator of the universe.

4. What are some ways a person might misuse Scripture in an attempt to discern God's will? Give examples.
There's a difference between knowing some verses of Scripture and under-standing the mind of God. This question is intended to highlight the importance of things like balance, context, and perspective when using Scripture to make decisions.

5. What are some proper ways to use Scripture to discern God's will? Give examples.
Following up on question 3, this question is designed to prompt sugges-tions of guidelines to ensure that Scripture is used in context and that other basic biblical principles are not overlooked in the process.

WHAT WILL YOU DO?
Similar to question 5 above, this exercise is intended to bring God's sovereignty front and center in our consciousness. The end goal is to cultivate a growing desire to read God's Word and to seek His will.

ADDITIONAL SUGGESTIONS:
Ask your group to share some experiences in which their perspectives were drasti-cally altered by the addition of information. Then challenge them to realize that if we possessed the information God possesses, we would never question His ways. That being the case, we can fully trust Him even though we don't know all the details.

SESSION 6 *Inside the Mind of God*

KEY POINT: *The way you think determines how you act or perform. If you think like a winner, you'll play like a winner. If you think like a professional, you'll perform like a professional. This basic principle about life also applies to your spiritual life. The more you think like God, the more you will begin to perform according to His will. And the way to learn God's mind and His ways is through study of the Scriptures.*

EXERCISE:
This exercise is intended to demonstrate the practice of recognizing principles from God's Word. Some are stated outright, and some are illustrated through parables or historical accounts. But sometimes the principle is merely implied. Encourage your group to be on the lookout for principles whenever they study Scripture.

VIDEO NOTES:
From the video message, fill in the blanks.

1. We have the opportunity, the honor, and the privilege to <u>renew</u> our minds and our thinking so that we think more like God.
2. Three areas where God's ways are higher than ours:
    a. <u>Relationships</u>
    b. <u>Finances</u>
    c. <u>Physical</u> life
3. In our thinking and in our praying, we've got to begin the <u>decision</u>-making process with this presupposition: my ways are not His ways, and my thoughts are not His thoughts.
4. A principle is an <u>unchangeable</u> truth.
5. Sometimes they describe a cause-and-effect <u>relationship</u>.
6. At other times they predict the <u>outcomes</u> of behaviors and attitudes.
7. You can disobey <u>commands</u>, but you don't disobey a principle.

Three Ways to Find Principles in the Scriptures:

8. Sometimes principles are <u>stated</u>.
9. Sometimes principles are just <u>implied</u>.
10. Sometimes principles are <u>illustrated</u> through narratives.
11. The more familiar we become with the principles of God's word, the easier it is to discern the <u>will</u> of God.
12. Every single decision you make is going to <u>cross</u> with one of the principles of God's Word.

NOTES FOR DISCUSSION QUESTIONS:
1. When we are not guided by God's principles, we typically resort to whatever our fears and desires lead us to do. What are some ways a person's fears might influence decision making? Give examples.
   The purpose of this question is to encourage awareness of our own fears and the way they impact our decisions.
2. What are some ways a person's desires might influence decision making? Give examples.
   Similar to question 1, only this time probing for desires that may steer us away from God's will.
3. Read Matthew 16:24. What does this passage suggest about the relationship between following God and discovering His will? Explain.
   To discover God's will, you must be willing to follow those components of His guidance and instruction that you already know.

ADDITIONAL CONVERSATION STARTERS:
4. Are you more likely to be influenced by fear or by desires? Explain.
   Similar to questions 1 and 2, the goal of this question is deeper introspection.
5. A protégé is someone who models himself after his superior. What people can you name from your past after whom you have modeled aspects of your life?
   This question will encourage people to realize that modeling themselves after another is a natural process and has probably been a part of their own past...perhaps without their awareness. By realizing this natural process, they will be more likely to embrace it as a concept for pursuing godliness.
6. How long would you have to be a student of God's Word before you could begin modeling yourself after Him? Discuss.
   There is no right or wrong answer here. Obviously, a person would have to possess some Bible knowledge; however, any point makes a good starting point.
7. What is the difference between recognizing someone's example and modeling yourself after someone? Discuss.
   The point of this question is that modeling their behavior might require some intentionality. It's not enough just to notice that God exists. We must spend time renewing our minds to the truths of His Word.

WHAT WILL YOU DO?
The point of this exercise is to foster the practice of recognizing principles from God's Word and applying them to everyday life.

ADDITIONAL SUGGESTIONS:
Unless something is in front of us on a daily basis, we tend to forget about it. Likewise, things we see and hear regularly are top-of-mind. Advertisers know this principle all too well. Ask your group to name some examples of this principle from everyday life.

SESSION 7 *The Big Picture*

KEY POINT: *One of the most significant ways God reveals His will is in the area of vision. When you are burdened by a particular issue and have a vision about the way things could be, there's a good possibility God could use that vision to compel you toward His will for your life.*

EXERCISE:
This exercise is intended to familiarize people with the process of developing a vision and to encourage them to approach the future thinking in terms of fulfilling a vision.

VIDEO NOTES:
From the video message, fill in the blanks.
1. One of the primary ways that God will direct you and guide you in life is by giving you a big-picture <u>vision</u> for your life.
2. A vision is basically a <u>destination</u>.
3. A vision is a mental image of what could be, fueled by the <u>conviction</u> that this is something that should be true of your life.
4. As the vision gets <u>clearer</u>, the options get <u>fewer</u>, and the decisions get <u>easier</u>.
5. Everybody has some <u>general</u> idea of where they want to end up in life.
6. As long as your vision is general, it is not <u>helpful</u>.
7. Only in the arenas where we have some semblance of a big <u>picture</u> do the options clarify themselves.
8. As a Christian, as you allow God to have <u>input</u> into this picture, it makes discerning His will so much easier.

NOTES FOR DISCUSSION QUESTIONS:
1. In which of the following categories are you personally most likely to have a vision? Rank them in order.
    __Career
    __Relationship with spouse
    __Friendships
    __Finances
    __Spiritual
    This question is designed to provoke self-exploration and the revelation that most people already experience vision in everyday life.
2. Have you ever been involved in a task that had a clear vision? Explain.

Drawing from personal experience, people will be encouraged to recall the value of vision.

3. Why is it important to write out goals or visions?
    The point of this question is to get everyone to agree that the act of writing out goals is important.

4. Read Ephesians 2:10. What does this passage say about God's vision for your life?
    God's vision for your life is intrinsically linked to specific works that He created you to perform, and He ordains the circumstances of the universe to come together at the appropriate points in time to support your fulfillment of His plan.

    ADDITIONAL CONVERSATION STARTERS:

5. Have you ever been involved in a task that did not have a clear vision? Explain.
    Similar to question 2, this question demonstrates the downside of operating without vision.

6. Compare and contrast the two experiences from questions 2 and 5.
    The goal of this question is to further examine the findings from questions 2 and 5.

7. What are some ways a vision might begin? Give examples.
    The purpose of this question is to sensitize people to things in their own lives that might represent a potential vision.

8. How can you tell if a vision is from God?
    This question is designed to remind us that not every vision is from God. We must also use prudence and wisdom before pursuing something we think is from God.

9. In your own words, describe the relationship between *vision* and *conviction*. Discuss.
    The greater the conviction, the clearer the vision (and vice versa).

10. What are some ways a *vision* is different from a *wish*? Discuss.
    A wish does not involve any action plan or concrete hope of materialization; it simply desires something. A vision, however, is always accompanied by a strategic mindset and a plan of execution.

WHAT WILL YOU DO?
This is yet another exercise to encourage people to develop vision. In particular, this exercise will demonstrate the value of developing a detailed vision in specific areas.

ADDITIONAL SUGGESTIONS:
Ask your group this question: Why do you think visions make such powerful motivators?

SESSION 8 *This One Thing*

KEY POINT: *Having vision is one thing. Maintaining vision is another. If a vision is to survive to fruition, it must be protected with vigilance and ferocity. The story of Nehemiah demonstrates how this man of God protected and maintained his vision in a very practical way.*

EXERCISE:
This exercise is intended to demonstrate how easily we can be pulled in one direction or another in life. The point of the lesson is that if you are not cautious and intentional about how you choose to apply yourself, there's no telling what direction your life might take.

VIDEO NOTES:
From the video message, fill in the blanks.
1. Nehemiah was the cupbearer to a king whose predecessors had destroyed <u>Israel</u>.
2. Nehemiah was about <u>800</u> miles away from Jerusalem.
3. A vision begins as a <u>burden</u>.
4. Nehemiah began to develop a vision for rebuilding the <u>walls</u> around Jerusalem.
5. Other <u>leaders</u> in the area were threatened by Nehemiah's plans.
6. Sanballat and his followers invited Nehemiah to meet them on the plain of <u>Ono</u>.
7. Nehemiah's response can be translated: "I am doing a great <u>work</u>, and I cannot come down."
8. For Nehemiah, anything that contributed to rebuilding the wall was a <u>yes</u>, and anything that would distract him from rebuilding the wall was a <u>no</u>.

Three Points of Application:
9. <u>Pray</u> that God will give you a vision for your life.
10. <u>Write</u> it down.
11. <u>Act</u> accordingly.

NOTES FOR DISCUSSION QUESTIONS:
1. Which of the following best describes how you ended up in your current job or occupation?
   a. Where I am today is part of a strategic plan I devised two or more jobs ago.

b. I have a plan for exactly what the next step in my career/occupation will be.
c. I have a general sense that this job will lead me where I want to go in life.
d. This job was a better offer than my last one, so I took it.
e. I have no idea why I'm here.

This question takes a look at how intentionally we approach life. Some people might be surprised to discover that they are not as strategic as they think.

2. Read Nehemiah 1:4. What was Nehemiah's first reaction to the news about the remnant in Jerusalem?
    Nehemiah sat down and wept. This question suggests that a certain level of emotional energy is required before something can be classified as a burden.

3. According to this passage, what did Nehemiah do before presenting his vision to God?
    Nehemiah mourned and fasted and prayed for "some days." This question is intended to underscore how seriously Nehemiah contemplated his burden as it progressed into a vision.

4. Read Nehemiah 2:1–5. What events did God use to give Nehemiah confirmation about his vision?
    In this passage, the king noticed Nehemiah's sadness and initiated the conversation. Two points are worth noting here: Nehemiah did not have an elaborate, contrived plan for making the king aware of his vision; he simply went about his business, sensitive to opportunities. And God used ordinary-looking circumstances to move the vision forward; often the people involved are unaware that their actions are part of the fulfillment of a long-term vision.

ADDITIONAL CONVERSATION STARTERS:

5. What would you say is the difference between an interest and a burden?
    We have stated that a vision begins as a burden. This question will help clarify what that means. Obviously, a burden involves much more concern than a passing interest. Before deciding that a burden should be a vision, you should first confirm that it is indeed a burden.

6. In your opinion, how long should someone wait before acting on a vision?
    There is no right or wrong answer to this question. The main point is that you should act prudently and be willing to be patient. God's timing is always perfect.

7. In your decision making, how much of the time are you consciously considering your long-term future?
    *   Always
    *   Mostly
    *   Sometimes
    *   Hardly
    *   Never

    The purpose of this question is to alert people to the presence or absence of intentionality in their own lives.

8. Have you ever written down specific goals for your life? How recently?

    The purpose of this question is to provoke self-exploration and a felt need for written goals and vision.

9. Is it a sin NOT to have a long-term plan in mind when you make a decision? Why or why not?

    There is no need for a conclusive answer to this question. It simply causes us to think through the importance of being sober and vigilant as we live out our days.

WHAT WILL YOU DO?
This exercise, conducted during the week, is intended to make people spend more time thinking about different areas in which God might be birthing a vision for their lives.

ADDITIONAL SUGGESTIONS:
Ask your group this question: What are some reasons why people are more productive and efficient when they are single-minded? Also, why are people sometimes so willing to entertain distractions that rob them of productivity and fulfillment?

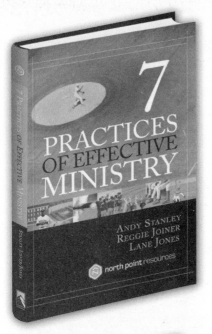

7 Practices of Effective Ministry

by Andy Stanley, Reggie Joiner, and Lane Jones
ISBN 1-59052-373-3

Rethink Your Ministry Game Plan

Succeeding in sports means victory, winning! But what does it mean in your ministry? An insightful and entertaining parable for every church leader who yearns for a more simplified approach to ministry.

Creating Community

by Andy Stanley and Bill Willits
ISBN 1-59052-396-2

Form Small Groups That Succeed

To build a healthy, thriving small-group environment you need a plan. Here are five proven principles from one of the most successful small-group ministry churches in the country. Learn them, implement them, and empower God's people to truly do life together.

north point resources

Parental Guidance Required
by Andy Stanley and Reggie Joiner
DVD: ISBN 1-59052-378-4
Study Guide: ISBN 1-59052-381-4

Influence Your Child's Future
Our lives are shaped by relationships, experiences, and decisions. Therefore, our priority as parents should be to enhance our child's relationship with us, advance our child's relationship with God, and influence our child's relationship with those outside the home.

Discovering God's Will
by Andy Stanley
DVD: ISBN 1-59052-380-6
Study Guide: ISBN 1-59052-379-2

Make Decisions with Confidence
God has a personal vision for your life and He wants you to know it even more than you do. Determining God's will can be a difficult process, especially when we need to make a decision in a hurry. In this series Andy Stanley leads us through God's providential, moral, and personal will.

The Best Question Ever
by Andy Stanley
DVD: ISBN 1-59052-463-2
Study Guide: ISBN 1-59052-462-4

Foolproof Your Life
When it comes to sorting out the complexities of each unique situation we face, only wisdom can reveal the best path. The question posed here will empower you to make regretless decisions every time.

north point resources

Taking Care of Business
by Andy Stanley
DVD: ISBN 1-59052-492-6
Study Guide: ISBN 1-59052-491-8

Finding God at Work
God created work and intends for us to make the most of it! Gain His perspective and get equipped to make changes that allow you to thrive in the workplace.

Life Rules
by Andy Stanley
DVD: ISBN 1-59052-494-2
Study Guide: ISBN 1-59052-493-4

Instructions for Life
God's guidelines for living are for your protection and freedom. Learn them, live by them, and experience the dramatic, positive change in every area of your life.

north point resources